Donald J. Trump 2020
Perfect Reelection Coloring Book

KM Graphics

First Printing: 2020

KM Graphics
P.O. Box 21906
Okla. City, OK 73156

THE CONTENDERS

IT'S GONNA BE
HUGE!

NO MORE

Fake News!

ACCOMPLISHMENTS

in only 3 years...

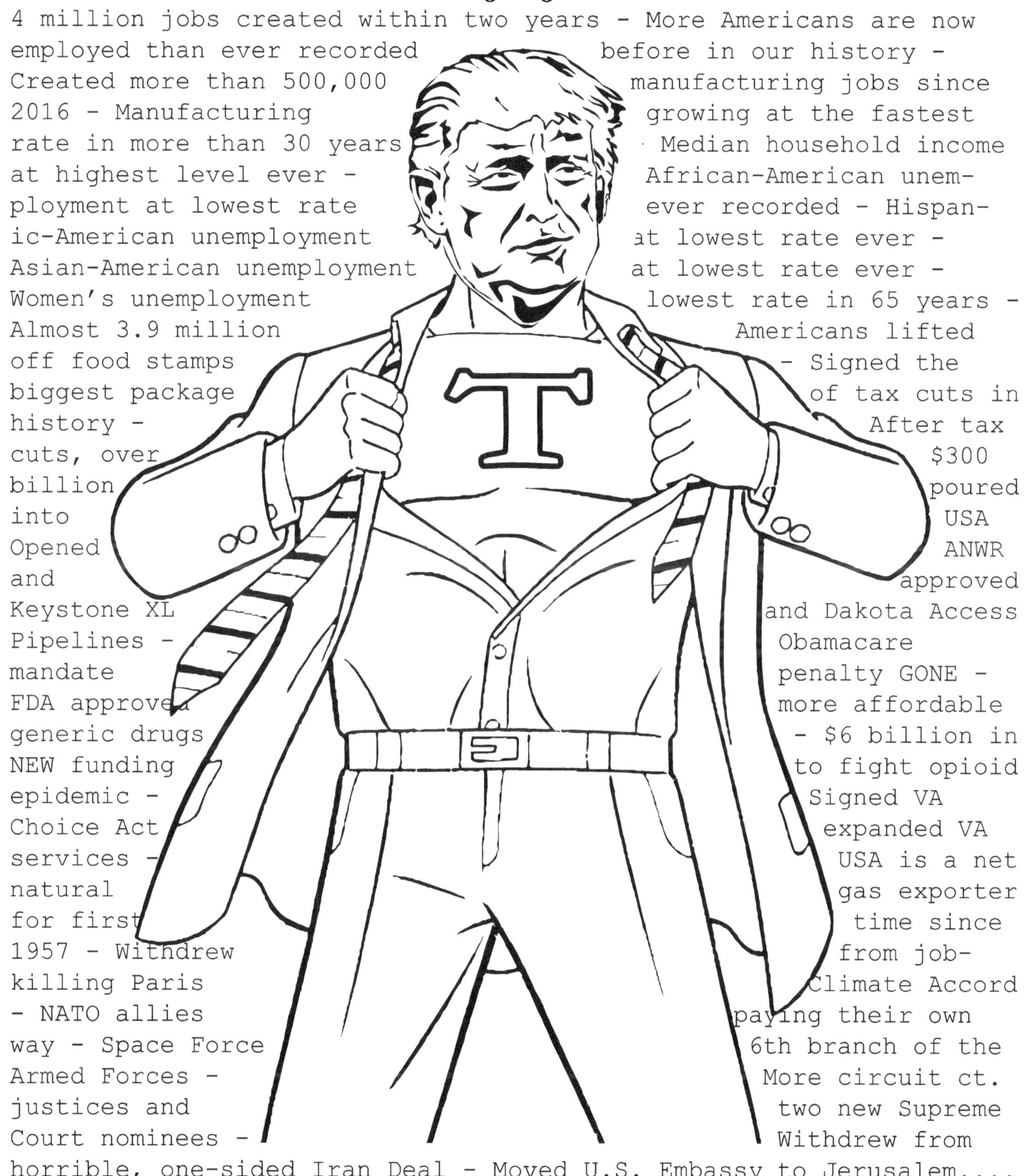

4 million jobs created within two years - More Americans are now employed than ever recorded before in our history - Created more than 500,000 manufacturing jobs since 2016 - Manufacturing growing at the fastest rate in more than 30 years Median household income at highest level ever - African-American unem- ployment at lowest rate ever recorded - Hispan- ic-American unemployment at lowest rate ever - Asian-American unemployment at lowest rate ever - Women's unemployment lowest rate in 65 years - Almost 3.9 million Americans lifted off food stamps - Signed the biggest package of tax cuts in history - After tax cuts, over $300 billion poured into USA Opened ANWR and approved Keystone XL and Dakota Access Pipelines - Obamacare mandate penalty GONE - FDA approved more affordable generic drugs - $6 billion in NEW funding to fight opioid epidemic - Signed VA Choice Act expanded VA services - USA is a net natural gas exporter for first time since 1957 - Withdrew from job- killing Paris Climate Accord - NATO allies paying their own way - Space Force 6th branch of the Armed Forces - More circuit ct. justices and two new Supreme Court nominees - Withdrew from horrible, one-sided Iran Deal - Moved U.S. Embassy to Jerusalem....

"We hold these truths to be self-evident. All men and women are created... by the... you know... you know the thing,"
Declaration of Independence
Sleepy Joe
rewrites history

A Rare Sighting of a Lying, Dog-faced, Pony Soldier in His Natural Habitat

Lemme Out!
I think it worked...

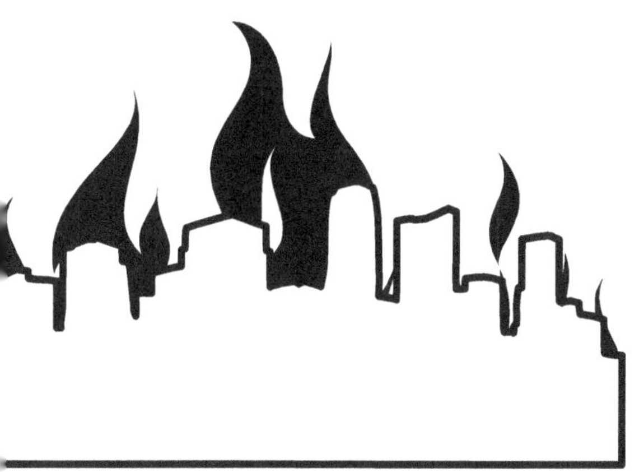

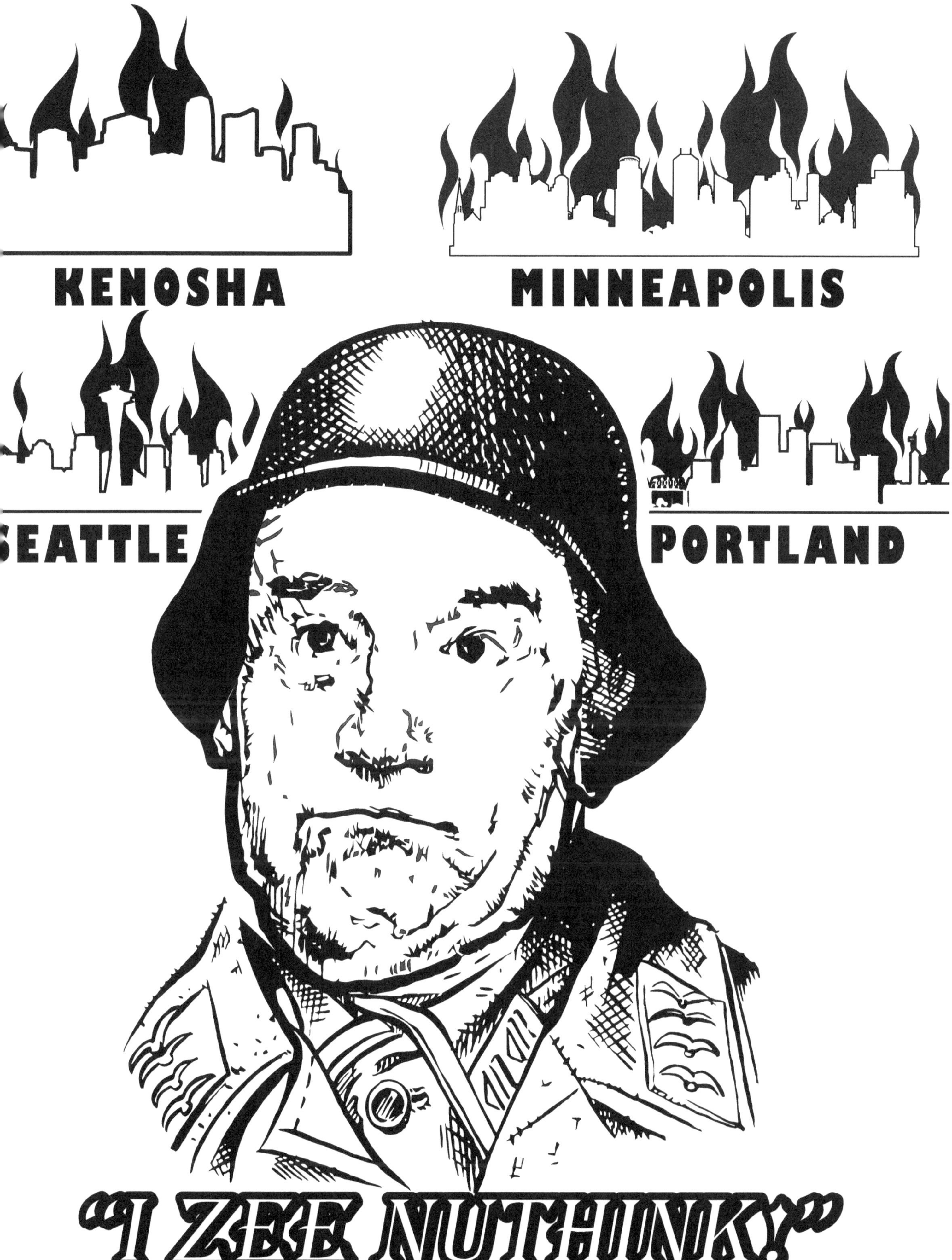
KENOSHA
MINNEAPOLIS
SEATTLE
PORTLAND
"I ZEE NUTHINK!"

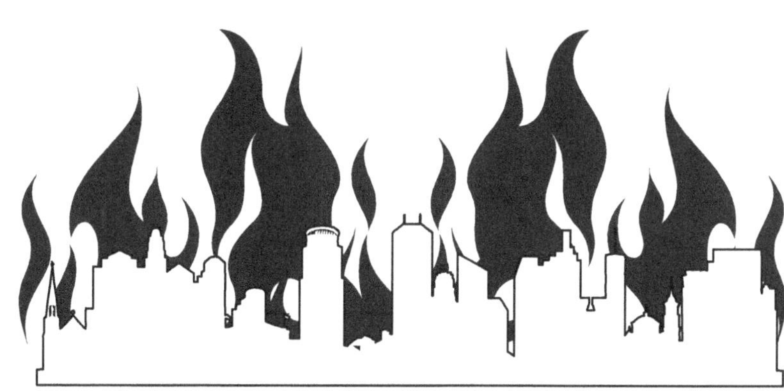

ACCOMPLISHMENTS

in 47 years...

- Opposed court ordered busing to desegregate public schools in 1970's
- Claimed in many speeches in the 80's to have marched in civil rights movement, but no evidence supports that claim
- Pulled out of first presidential bid in 1987 for plagiarizing speech and falsely claiming his ancestors worked in the coal mines.
- Voted against the liberation of Kuwait in 1991.
- Voted for Iraq war in 2002
- Dropped out of second presidential bid in 2008 after coming in last in Iowa
- In 2014 as VP, got youngest son, Hunter, a job with Burisma though he had no experience or qualifications
- In 2015, got prosecutor in investigation of Burisma fired
- Until 2020 in S. Carolina, Joe Biden had never won any delegates in any state in any of his three bids for president

THE LOSERS

Bernie and Friends

...with great schools

HARVARD
LAW
FAUXCAHONTAS

The Noise

Schiff Hits the Fan

Nan the Ripper

"Unemployment benefits are creating jobs faster than practically any other program..."
"Every month that we do not have an economic recovery package 500 million Americans lose their jobs."
"But we have to pass the bill so you can find out what is in it..."
MME SPEAKER

Neurotic Nancy

THE FUTURE?
THE BOLSHEVIXENS

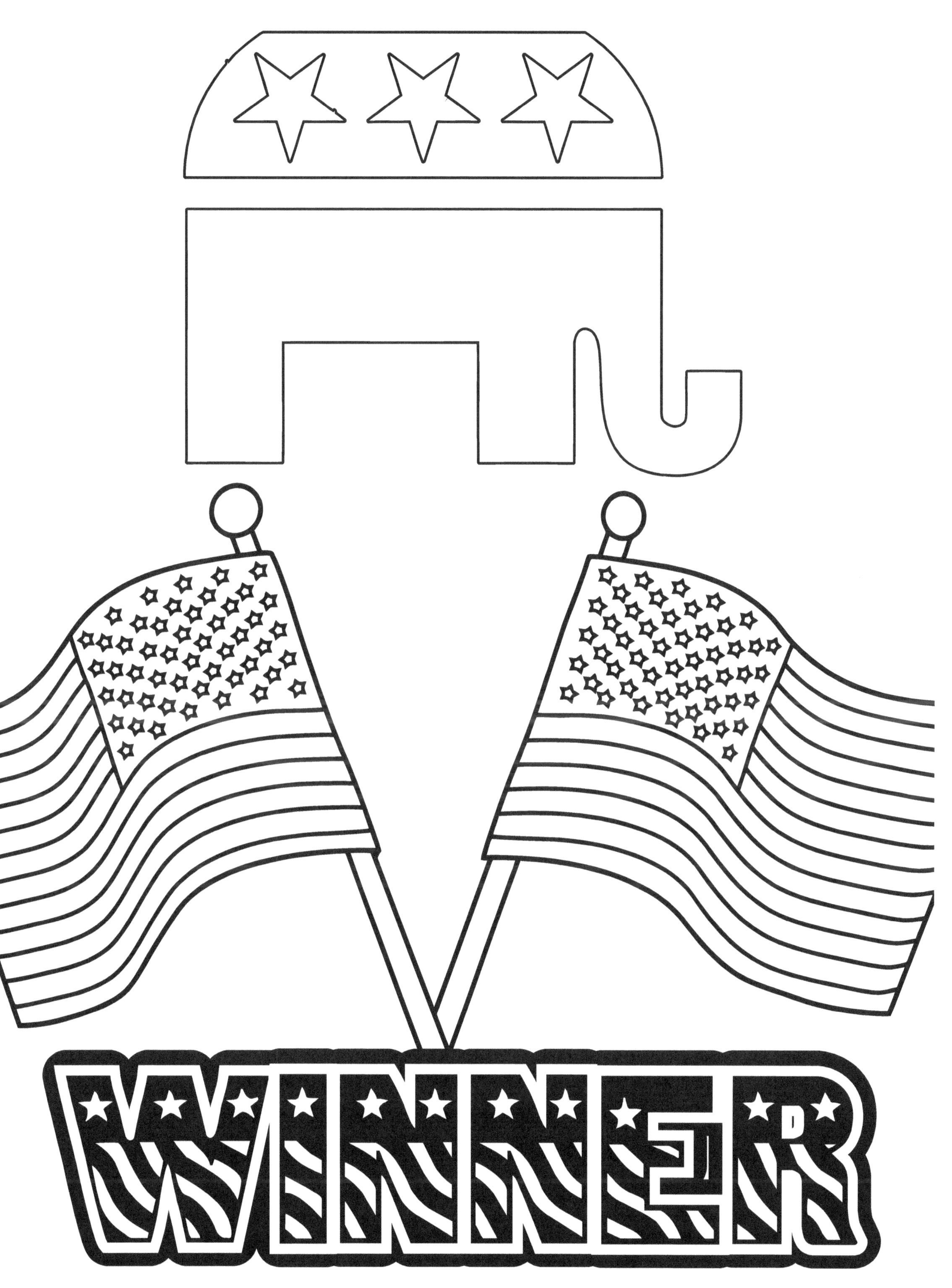
WINNER

4 MORE YEARS!

"I mean, we're talking a perfect election. When they look back at history, books will be written on how perfect a campaign we ran. There's never been a more perfect campaign, never will be a more perfect campaign in our country ever again... almost as perfect as this coloring book!"